WHAT'S NEXT? Getting Ahead of Change

MMPT Option A **MMPT Option B** **MMPT Option C**

Cover image: This rendering depicts one of three concept designs for the Georgia Department of Transportation's MultiModal Passenger Terminal (MMPT) project. The project is a transportation hub that will provide a central linkage for existing and planned transit services. All three concepts are being considered and there is no preferred design. Project partners include the Metropolitan Atlanta Rapid Transit Authority (MARTA), the Atlanta Regional Commission, the Georgia Regional Transportation Authority, Central Atlanta Progress, the Atlanta Downtown Improvement District, the city of Atlanta, and a host of community and private interests working together to carry out the project.
Credit: Renderings courtesy of FIC
Architects: FXFOWLE in association with Cooper Carry

© 2012 Urban Land Institute
1025 Thomas Jefferson Street, NW, Suite 500 West
Washington, DC 20007-5201

Printed in the United States of America. All rights reserved. No part of this book may be reproduced in any form or by any means, electronic or mechanical, including photocopying and recording, or by any information storage or retrieval system, without written permission of the publisher.

Recommended Bibliographic Listing:
Urban Land Institute. *What's Next? Getting Ahead of Change*. Washington, D.C.: Urban Land Institute, 2012

International Standard Book Number: 978-0-87420-218-2

SUPPORT AND SPONSORSHIP

The Urban Land Institute gratefully acknowledges the leadership and support of UDR, Inc.

UDR, Inc. (NYSE:UDR), an S&P 400 company, is a leading multifamily real estate investment trust with a demonstrated performance history of delivering superior and dependable returns by successfully managing, buying, selling, developing, and redeveloping attractive real estate properties in targeted U.S. markets. UDR is honored to celebrate with ULI its 75th commemorative year. As a proud long-term sponsor of ULI, we recognize the industry-leading research, education, and community outreach efforts of ULI and its goal of providing participants with thoughtful analysis, spirited debate, and industry best practices. UDR is grateful for the forum ULI has provided the Company to facilitate the open exchange of ideas and information as well as the sharing of experience with other local, national, and multinational industry leaders.

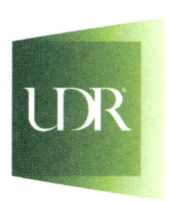

The Urban Land Institute recognizes the following supporters as ULI 75th Anniversary sponsors:

Allen Matkins
Bank of America Merrill Lynch
Caruso Affiliated
CBRE
Cisco
Eastdil Secured
Ernst & Young — Quality In Everything We Do
HFF — Holliday Fenoglio Fowler, L.P.
IPA Institutional Property Advisors — A Marcus & Millichap Company
Jones Lang LaSalle — Real value in a changing world
KB Home
Kennedy Wilson — thriving on opportunity
Kilroy Realty Corporation
KTR Capital Partners
LBA Realty
Lincoln Property Company
MacFarlane Partners
Majestic Realty Co.
Marcus & Millichap Real Estate Investment Services
Oaktree
Prologis
Sares·Regis Group
UDR
Union Bank
U.S. Bank
Wells Fargo

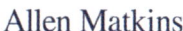

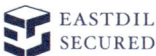

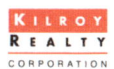

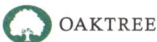

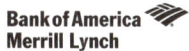

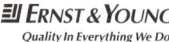

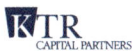

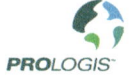

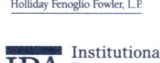

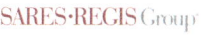

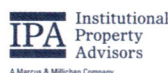

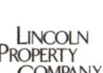

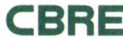

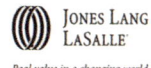

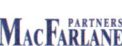

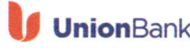

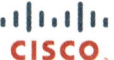

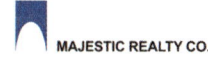

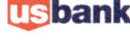

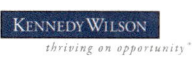

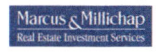

ABOUT THE URBAN LAND INSTITUTE

The Urban Land Institute is a 501(c)(3) nonprofit research and education organization supported by its members. Founded in 1936, the Institute now has members in 95 countries worldwide, representing the entire spectrum of land use and real estate development disciplines working in private enterprise and public service.

As the preeminent, multidisciplinary real estate forum, ULI facilitates an open exchange of ideas, information, and experience among local, national, and international industry leaders and policy makers dedicated to creating better places.

The mission of the Urban Land Institute is to provide leadership in the responsible use of land and in creating and sustaining thriving communities worldwide. ULI is committed to

- Bringing together leaders from across the fields of real estate and land use policy to exchange best practices and serve community needs;
- Fostering collaboration within and beyond ULI's membership through mentoring, dialogue, and problem solving;
- Exploring issues of urbanization, conservation, regeneration, land use, capital formation, and sustainable development;
- Advancing land use policies and design practices that respect the uniqueness of both built and natural environments;
- Sharing knowledge through education, applied research, publishing, and electronic media; and
- Sustaining a diverse global network of local practice and advisory efforts that address current and future challenges.

ULI's priorities are

- Promoting intelligent densification and urbanization;
- Creating resilient communities;
- Understanding demand and market forces;
- Connecting capital and the built environment through value; and
- Integrating energy, resources, and uses sustainably.

CONTENTS

- **6** LETTER
- **8** INTRODUCTION
- **14** SCALE UP (or down)
- **26** STAY CLOSE
- **36** MAKE OVER
- **46** JUMP AHEAD
- **58** KEEP WATCH
- **68** LEADING TO NEXT

DEAR READER:

The Urban Land Institute kicked off its 75th anniversary celebration at the 2011 ULI Fall Meeting with a new dialogue spurred on by the anniversary publication, *What's Next? Real Estate in the New Economy*. Since then, *Real Estate in the New Economy* has been the catalyst for programs in councils and meetings across the Institute. By engaging in this dialogue, ULI members celebrate the past by looking forward and shaping the future. It is our great honor to mark the conclusion to the 75th anniversary and simultaneously kick off ULI's next 75 years of mission-driven engagement by issuing this sequel publication, *What's Next? Getting Ahead of Change*.

With a legacy rooted in a handful of landowners sharing best practices during the Great Depression, ULI has grown to nearly 30,000 members worldwide, with over 65 District and Country Councils and over 50 Product Councils. A nonprofit organization with headquarters in Washington, D.C., and regional offices in London and Hong Kong, ULI has become the premier source of multidisciplinary research and education in the real estate and urban development industry.

Serving investors, lenders, developers, owners, service providers, and public officials alike, ULI is a safe haven where market participants engage in dialogue, analysis, and debate to review market trends, best practices, and future challenges faced by local communities and their markets. ULI has become one of the most localized global organizations in the world.

Last year's anniversary publication, *Real Estate in the New Economy*, showed us that we are indeed surrounded by wholesale change. This publication, *Getting Ahead of Change*, shows us that organizations and communities are successfully responding to a new set of market drivers.

As we forge ahead through uncertain markets further into the 21st century, the ULI network positions its members not only as better professionals in the real estate and urban development marketplace, but also as industry leaders and community builders.

As the single largest and most widespread financial asset class in the world, real estate is central to global economic recovery and to sustaining thriving communities. We hope the ULI network and this publication spur you to get ahead of change.

Sincerely,

Peter S. Rummell
Chairman

Patrick L. Phillips
Chief Executive Officer

INTRODUCTION

AMID CHRONIC AMBIGUITY, CHANGE BECOMES THE ACCEPTED CONSTANT, CHALLENGING CONVENTION LIKE NEVER BEFORE.
SO, WHAT'S NEXT? HOW CAN YOU **THRIVE** IN THIS DECADE'S UNSETTLED MARKETS?

ARE YOU READY? With one camp of economists predicting another rocky year or two transitioning to a decade of calmer markets and steady growth, and a second camp believing that market upheaval and uncertainty are here to stay, leaders in real estate must be ready to alter how they do business in lean times and seize new opportunities as they arise. Will there ever be a "new normal"?

As the industry stays lean and works harder to produce profit, its underlying resilience and entrepreneurial creativity will get put to the test. As the cost and complexity of projects increase, the market's willingness—or its ability—to pay may decline. Markets within

IN 2011, ULI published *What's Next? Real Estate in the New Economy*, highlighting a combination of economic trends driving changes in the real estate industry and sounding a cautionary note about past ways of doing business:

WORK Where the hell are the jobs? As the economy slowly recovers, jobs continue to cluster in and around gateways and rely more on growth in professional services, including the education and health care sectors.

LIVE What and where do you call home? Urban lifestyles seem more alluring and practical, and the housing bust creates opportunities for apartment developers and investors.

CONNECT Of what value is proximity? The best and most sought-after locations remain the most convenient, but information technology can make location irrelevant.

RENEW Where does your energy come from? From building design to locational preferences and neighborhood planning, opportunities exist to reduce energy costs and enhance property values.

MOVE How will transportation define market value? Time is money—the less we spend stuck in traffic and the more efficiently we travel between where we live, work, and play, the greater the value we put on location and place.

INVEST Where will growth, value, and risk come from? Investors need greater discipline and more knowledge to be successful. Clever financial products and diversification strategies may not offer protection against underlying risks as commercial real estate players operate across global markets.

> "Today we stand in a special place of responsibility as we witness a magnitude of changes that could transform society over the course of a single decade. We must understand these trends if we are to create durable value."
>
> **PETER RUMMELL,**
> CHAIRMAN, ULI, AT 2012 ULI SPRING MEETING IN CHARLOTTE, NORTH CAROLINA

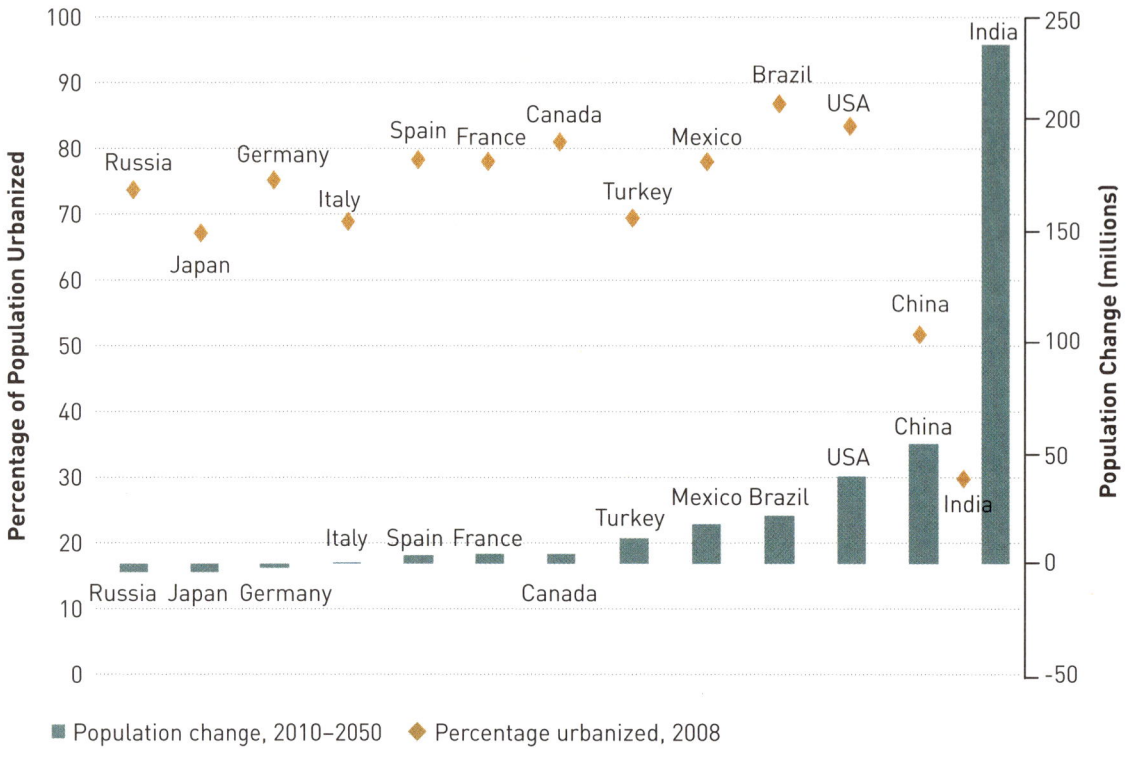

POPULATION GROWTH AND URBANIZATION: THE ROAD AHEAD (2010–2025)

■ Population change, 2010–2050   ◆ Percentage urbanized, 2008

Sources: United Nations Department of Economic and Social Affairs, World Population Prospects; CIA, World Factbook.

Whereas India and China move through a dramatic transition to become more urbanized societies, the United States is the market that is both highly urbanized and growing rapidly in population.

individual property sectors will fragment into more niches, where location, floor plates, and operations become the fundamental variables of product customization. Understanding—and anticipating—tenant needs becomes crucial to success as technology, demographics, and financial realities all combine to disrupt local markets. Real estate professionals, organizations, and communities will make choices either to lead the changes ahead or to hang back and ride the markets.

The market trends explored in last year's *What's Next? Real Estate in the New Economy* will continue to roil the property landscape in communities for the foreseeable future, especially in light of North America's economic slowdown, Europe's fiscal swoon, ongoing turmoil in the Middle East, and growth hiccups in Brazil, China, Russia,

and other emerging market champions. As these macroeconomic drivers touch down in local communities, their impacts blend with local undercurrents related to aging populations, unprepared workforces, or the disruption caused by information technologies. And all variables associated with strategic real estate investment must be reassessed and then reassessed again.

This sequel publication, *What's Next? Getting Ahead of Change*, synthesizes a spectrum of dialogue across ULI spurred by the first publication and explores how individuals, organizations, and communities are striking out in new directions in their efforts to embrace market realities, leverage new trends, and sustain thriving communities.

Drexel University's new campus plan embraces both existing buildings and the surrounding neighborhood through the creation of high-quality public spaces and repositioned retail uses. By working with a host of public and private interests, Drexel and the University of Pennsylvania are catalyzing $2 billion of real estate investment in Philadelphia.

REAL MEAN HOUSEHOLD INCOME, CUMULATIVE GROWTH BY QUINTILE

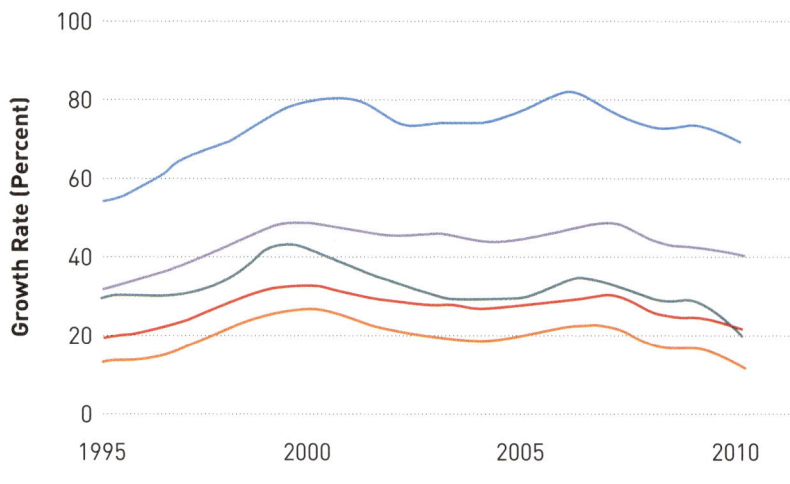

Source: U.S. Census Bureau.

Diverse growth in income and purchasing power in the United States forms one aspect of the economic backdrop for market preferences, purchasing decisions, and housing policy.

Together, these strategies add up to a new orientation for the real estate and urban development industry. It is a market stance in which individual professions, real estate products, and the professional practices of the past may need to be refined or reinvented to embrace a new generation of value creation:

SCALE UP (OR DOWN) The real estate industry embraces niche markets in a global marketplace. Scale up to capture new markets or scale down to dominate specialized knowledge, but don't get caught in the middle of a wave of market consolidation.

STAY CLOSE Whether situated on global pathways or nestled in local patterns, value is found in the context. New opportunities may be closer than you think.

MAKE OVER In a culture of embracing the "new," it is time for real estate players to find value across existing assets. Value can be achieved through efficiencies and reinvention, as old buildings get made over to become new.

JUMP AHEAD We know the trends and can estimate the timelines. It is up to real estate players to pull it all together and anticipate the kinds of buildings and spaces that future communities will need.

"As a physical asset with the ability to provide income and hedge against inflation, real estate becomes an attractive proposition when compared to many other asset classes. A new combination of factors presents numerous new opportunities for those with the ability and experience to take advantage of them."

PIERRE VAQUIER, CEO, AXA REIM

KEEP WATCH Just when you thought the real estate industry was maturing and becoming too predictable, a new set of risk variables undermined value. Whether internal or external, local or global, or public or private, real estate professionals need to keep watch for and price a new spectrum of risk.

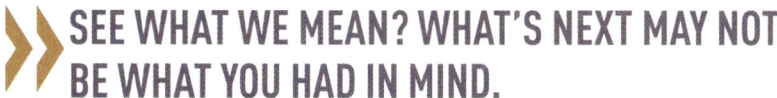

SEE WHAT WE MEAN? WHAT'S NEXT MAY NOT BE WHAT YOU HAD IN MIND.

SCALE UP (or down)

WHAT ARE THE BOUNDARIES

SCALE UP (or down)

WHAT ARE THE **BOUNDARIES** OF YOUR MARKETS?

WHO IS YOUR **CUSTOMER**?

WILL YOU GROW **VERTICALLY OR HORIZONTALLY**?

THE ERA OF LESS—our decade of slower growth—does not limit possibility for those managing real estate decisions. As design, development, construction, and brokerage companies continue to expand their boundaries and scale—extending internationally through acquisitions or forging new market inroads—while others downsize to dominate a niche market or product type in order to find clarity and overcome uncertainty.

LESS MAY BE MORE

Over the long term, real estate has given investors high single-digit returns—about 75 percent from income, the remaining 25 percent from appreciated value. The era of easy credit helped leverage returns to unsustainable levels. But now, in the wake of the bust, returns will migrate back to more normalized ranges, maintaining an attractive spread above Treasuries. Fund managers who tout the potential for big opportunistic returns sound less convincing today. They may gain greater credibility and seem more prescient by promising less in an ongoing slow-growth economy, even though many institutions crave higher returns to fill yawning liability gaps.

Lower returns mean smaller promotes. Boutique fund managers that depend on financial structuring to boost returns will retreat from the market. They lack the platforms to cope with hands-on asset management. Increasingly, smaller operators will establish joint ventures or share services to compete in the marketplace rather than

> "It is better to share the equity than try to get all the upside by making foolhardy commitments. Today, financiers are not in a position to drive the market anymore. True real estate professionals have the opportunity to come back to the fore."
>
> **JEREMY NEWSUM,**
> IMMEDIATE PAST CHAIRMAN, ULI, AND EXECUTIVE TRUSTEE, THE GROSVENOR ESTATE, AT 2012 ULI SPRING MEETING IN CHARLOTTE, NORTH CAROLINA

MULTIFAMILY ON THE MOVE

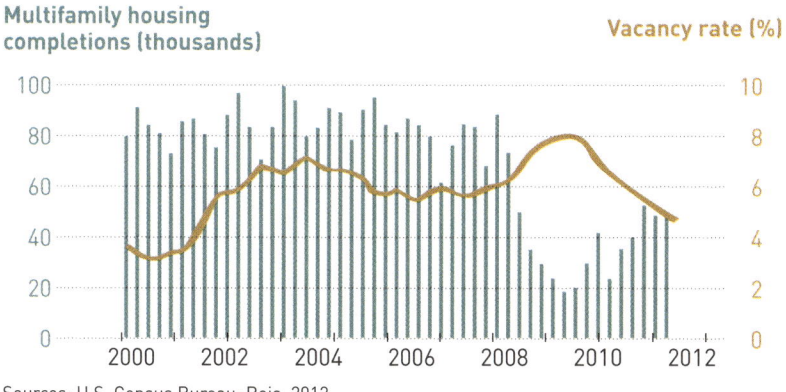

Sources: U.S. Census Bureau; Reis, 2012.

TORRID GROWTH

This decade represents Asia's steepest rate of urbanization over its century of transformation from 1950 to 2050. The top ten fastest-growing large cities in the world are all in China, representing growth in commercial office space alone of over 10 percent annually. As urban development and real estate service providers strive to create global brands, international business practices and sophisticated investors overcome traditional international market barriers. What is your Asia strategy?

Focus on:

CHENGDU With a metropolitan regional population of 14 million, the capital of Sichuan Province is reframing urban development by attracting new investment while simultaneously reconstructing neighborhoods damaged by the 2008 earthquake. Investments in higher-quality housing and newly diversified infrastructure are complemented by a 15 percent rise in GDP in 2011. The subway system inaugurated in 2009 continues to be expanded, while 1,772 kilometers of fiber-optic trunk lines support a burgeoning IT cluster. ULI's annual *China Cities Survey* ranked Chengdu as the country's most attractive city for investment, particularly in the apartment and retail sectors.

Public policy objectives drive the rapid development of subsidized housing in nearly all cities in China.

MANILA Famously dense, the city is making strides to refurbish infrastructure, while the Philippines works to build capacity in the capital markets.

HO CHI MINH CITY Vietnam's largest city plans to deliver a new six-line subway system between 2014 and 2020.

staff expensive new platforms. Big financial advisors must determine whether they are willing to bankroll people-intensive businesses with lowered margins and less profit pop in order to take advantage of bigger volumes. Managers of big, popular, and asset-rich core real estate funds seem best positioned; they garner handsome, annuity-like fees from managing assets for income-oriented returns during periods of long-term holds.

POWER OF SCALE

Bigger institutions, represented by large pension and sovereign wealth funds, will gravitate to those global gateway markets that are perceived to be safer places, where giant financial aggregators deploy most of their allocations in large increments—buying or holding the major office towers, apartment projects, and industrial parks—driving down capitalization rates. That leaves smaller local players (developers, regional banks, and property managers) to dominate secondary and tertiary markets where transaction activity remains more restrained. Investors cannot count on easy exits and returns rely much more on income flows than appreciation.

GROWING CLUSTERS GLOBALLY

And then consider the power of urban economic clusters. Cities will become favored again, because they conveniently cluster businesses and professional services together. Some clusters are more powerful than others: the brainpower clusters like Silicon Valley and the London financial district are magnets for globalized capital and high-paying jobs. Hospital centers draw significant commerce—research labs, medical offices, and plenty of patients—while major universities attract international students and companies, and encourage startups, which feed off professorial and student talent. Prime shopping districts (from Worth Avenue to the leading fortress regional malls) have always successfully drawn together the best retailers and command the highest sales per square foot. That won't change. And—no surprise—international airports and ports cluster the most valuable distribution space. Finding and creating clusters always pays in real estate, but identifying smaller niches and catering to them will reap rewards, too. One size doesn't fit all anymore.

> "We see the rise of megaregions around the world which grow denser as they outperform traditional single-city markets."
>
> **RICHARD FLORIDA,**
> ULI SENIOR VISITING FELLOW

ULI DISTRICT COUNCIL SURVEY

The shift to high-tech and medical business clusters will persist. Economically successful regions will be able to recruit faculty and students interested in technology transfer and commercial development of their research.

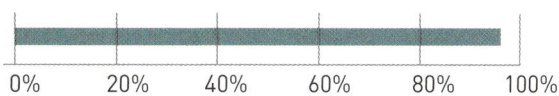

Source: ULI survey of U.S. District Councils, summer 2012.

LOCAL EXPERTISE ON A GLOBAL STAGE

The concentration of know-how in select U.S. cities is old news. But as "expert communities" learn to succeed globally, the power of globalization will be felt locally. As economic clusters go global, secondary and tertiary impacts help drive housing markets and investments in education and medical institutions that are fueling neighborhood development and demand for professional services. Even if corporate headquarters continue to favor leafy and secure locations, professional services will be delivered from mixed-use business districts.

Focus on:

HOUSTON With low vacancy rates and baseline growth in new real estate product uninterrupted since 2008, Houston's energy, medical, and high-technology cluster looms large on the global stage. As ExxonMobil consolidates its operations into a new global headquarters just south of The Woodlands, city leaders have helped nurture strong links with oil-producing regions of the world. This economic power and dynamism is seen in the population: Houston has enjoyed the fastest job and population growth in the country since 2007.

BAY AREA Silicon Valley casts a virtual shadow on the world as Apple, Facebook, Google, eBay, and

The new Exxon Mobil headquarters in Houston, Texas.

Twitter build out new corporate headquarters or retrofit existing buildings. San Jose's GDP jumped 13 percent from 2007 to 2010 and gen-Y knowledge workers choose South of Market over the suburbs.

BOSTON World-renowned institutions drive one-eighth of the Boston region's economic output, and the city ranks third in recent job creation—ahead of far larger Los Angeles.

USING LESS SPACE

As businesses shrink the amount of space per employee (smaller is better; that is, more profitable) and let more people work away from the office, they also may find that bigger floor plates can make it possible to shoehorn workforces more productively. Developers in major gateway cities take note: new cutting-edge towers (with expansive layouts and plenty of floor-to-ceiling natural light and under-floor air) should attract major tenants who can reduce their overall square footage in more efficient space.

Younger office workers do not aspire to corner offices with cushy living room sets and walnut credenzas. As long as they have confer-

Driven by new norms in the workplace, Nokia's new offices in Silicon Valley provide an open café-like environment for a workforce that may or may not be in the office on any given day.

ence and break space big enough to congregate and mingle, they willingly tolerate smaller personal work areas and less privacy. Designers are becoming increasingly creative about modifying cubicles into work benches and providing small conference rooms that allow private conversations in less private environments.

CHANGES IN SPACE PER OFFICE WORKER

	United States	New York	San Francisco
Current space allocation (square feet per job)	116	265	242
Current vacancy rate (%)	17	9	14
Scenario 1: Reduce 10 square feet per job			
New space allocation (square feet per job)	106	255	232
New vacancy rate (%)	24	12	18
Scenario 2: Reduce by 20 square feet per job			
New space allocation (square feet per job)	96	245	222
New vacancy rate (%)	31	16	21

Sources: BLS; CBRE-EA RREEF Research, as of Q1 2011.

SHRINKING INTO SHOWROOMS

Retailers are reducing space needs and operating costs, giving up large store displays with wide arrays of merchandise, and styling smaller showrooms supported by kiosks for ordering from wider selections online. Smaller formats and internet strategies allow big-box retail stores to penetrate into more urban locations, where developers fashion multilevel malls to accommodate them or adapt large and underused basement space in office towers.

SOME LIVING SMALL

The gen-Y cohort also settles for smaller (even tiny) residences in bigger cities and denser, mixed-use, 24-hour suburban centers, just as many of their baby boomer parents downsize into apartments or townhouses from bigger house-and-yard lifestyles in the suburbs. These empty nesters want to move closer to their career-building children, and they fancy taking care of less space. In the wealth islands where space commands premium pricing, tenants give up square footage to be closer to cultural amenities and lifestyle conveniences—an apartment can work if there is a park nearby and plenty of restaurants down the block. Architects and designers make their mark with creative solutions for storage space, lighting, and fold-up furnishings—sofas doubling as beds and desks turning into dining tables. Cities explore pilot zoning programs for "micro" apartment units—only 275 to 300 square feet—to help overcome a chronic

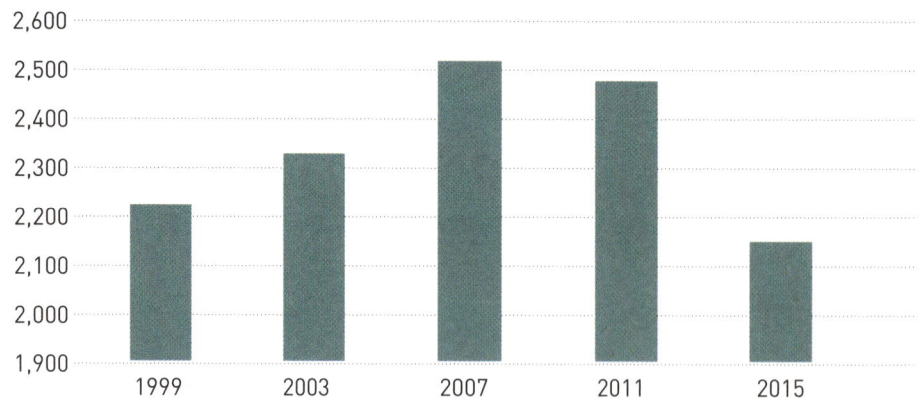

AVERAGE NEW HOME SIZE (SQUARE FEET)

Sources: The Demand Institute; U.S. Census Bureau; National Association of Homebuilders; Conference Board (consumer survey conducted in December 2011).

housing shortage. Mixed-use developers seek to provide ever more amenities, and the self-storage industry gets a boost because more people need a place to keep stuff that does not fit in their housing.

NAME THAT NICHE

The market will subdivide into niches with greater richness and complexity. Just examine the 60-plus cohort: While the overall numbers are growing, many new retirees will have fewer resources in the way of savings. Will they age in place and seek independence, or move in with relatives or friends? Downsize to an apartment in their neighborhood or look for a cheaper home in a warm place? The answer will be all of the above. The more affluent may downsize

The push to deliver affordable housing to new market niches is creating new formats for multifamily housing. The **SMARTSPACE**® project meets the aspirations of urban living by providing small studio apartments—300 square feet or less—in an outstanding location in the heart of San Francisco's South of Market neighborhood.

Next Gen℠–The Home Within a Home℠ floor plan reflects Lennar's next new attempt to provide flexible living space to an evolving residential marketplace made up of more intergenerational households, formed as the population ages and foreign-born or international buyers enter certain markets.

> "Our culture includes welcoming newcomers. It doesn't matter where you came from. If you want to pitch in, we will find a place for you."
>
> **HUGH McCOLL,**
> FORMER CHAIRMAN, BANK OF AMERICA, AT 2012 ULI SPRING MEETING IN CHARLOTTE, NORTH CAROLINA

from suburbs to city or decamp to a remote dream home destination. By sheer numbers, more people will build demand for senior communities, but some may want to live closer to select hospitals and doctors or to their children, while others will choose suburban lifestyles—townhouses and granny flats, preferably with easy-to-take-care-of layouts and not too many stairs.

BIGGER MAY WORK

Despite the trend toward less square feet per capita, larger residences can still work—even those much-maligned McMansions—if properly marketed at appropriate price points. Bigger suburban homes could be well suited to cost-cutting families and to immigrants looking to pool resources and live together in extended intergenerational units—parents, grandparents, and young-adult children can still collectively downsize out of multiple homes. Anticipating this trend, some homebuilders are designing new "home-within-home" projects with multiple entrances to separate suites. The different generations gain privacy with the benefits of shared space. Working couples, using separate home offices, may like this arrangement too.

More unrelated adults will share space, and suburban houses with multiple bedrooms can meet their needs. But these arrangements will more likely involve renters, not owners. For investors in single-family homes, managing these housing arrangements could present challenges and headaches in dealing with comings and goings. Residential brokers may profit from specializing in a new niche of property management.

RIGHTSIZING PROFESSIONS

What became too big and then too small will revert toward the mean. The more sedate transaction environment—no longer amped by easy credit and constrained by increasing regulation—will orient real estate careers toward less sexy and less remunerative bread-and-butter management and leasing. Middlemen brokers, appraisers, and lawyers will make a comeback, but gains in their numbers and compensation will be tempered by moderate market activity. Developers, homebuilders, and architects will expand again as population growth pushes demand for housing, but they will need to orient themselves to providing space that meets the needs of more frugal and efficient lifestyles. Specialization in smaller niche sectors likely will be more profitable and accepted than the standardized commodity developments of the past. For the near term at least, the United States and Europe do not need more tract housing or shopping center strips. For that action, players must move to underserved Latin America, Asia, and parts of Africa.

>> **SMALLER MAY MAKE MORE SENSE, BUT BIGGER RETAINS ITS ADVANTAGES.**

"If people whose money we're investing can't find the given city on the map, it's hard for them to get comfortable with that investment. But even so, this may not reflect the market fundamentals of the opportunity. Partner selection and trust is key."

RICHARD T.G. PRICE,
COCHAIRMAN, ULI ASIA PACIFIC, AND CHIEF EXECUTIVE, CBRE GLOBAL INVESTORS, AT 2012 ULI PAN ASIA DEVELOPMENT CONFERENCE IN BEIJING, CHINA

STAY CLOSE

HOW DOES YOUR PROJECT CONNECT

STAY CLOSE

HOW DOES YOUR PROJECT **CONNECT** TO YOUR COMMUNITY?

WHAT IS THE **CONTEXT** FOR CREATING VALUE?

TECHNOLOGY ALLOWS PEOPLE to work from just about anywhere. But look at just 30 global gateway cities, and you are looking at the markets in which nearly half of all institutional investment in real estate is placed. Business, commerce, and wealth concentrate in discrete locations like never before—a relatively small group of well-established global cities and other metropolitan areas where real estate investors naturally cluster.

Why? The proximity to business leaders and government policy makers, to cultural institutions, media centers, leading universities, and research hospitals. These places are knowledge networks and magnets for face-to-face deal making, money sourcing, decision making, and career building. In attracting top minds and talent, these communities create dynamic networks, where people willingly pay more to live, to work, and to own real estate assets. And in the

> "The millennial generation is much more interested in the experience of sharing than ownership. This is a profound trend and we are only in the early phases of it."
>
> **STEVE CASE,** CHAIRMAN AND CEO, REVOLUTION, AT ULI'S HONOR AWARD CEREMONY AT THE NATIONAL BUILDING MUSEUM IN WASHINGTON, D.C.

WORLD'S BUSIEST AIRPORT NODES

Rank	System (airports)	Passengers
1	London (LHR, LGW, LCY, STN, SEN, LTN)	127,353,419
2	New York (JFK, EWR, LGA, HPN, SWF, ISP)	107,586,717
3	Tokyo (HND, NRT)	98,024,708
4	Atlanta (ATL)	89,331,622
5	Paris (CDG, ORY)	86,203,669
6	Chicago (ORD, MDW)	84,302,427
7	Los Angeles (LAX, LGB, SNA, ONT, BUR)	79,981,524
8	Beijing (PEK, NAY)	76,171,801
9	Shanghai (PVG, SHA)	71,684,808
10	Dallas-Ft. Worth (DFW, DAL)	64,867,419
11	Miami (MIA, FLL, PBI)	63,998,275
12	Washington (IAD, DCA, BWI)	63,633,817
13	San Francisco (SFO, SJC, OAK)	56,905,161
14	Frankfurt (FRA, HHN)	56,172,796
15	Denver (DEN)	52,211,242
16	Seoul (ICN, GMP)	51,044,826
17	Moscow (DOM, SVO, VKO)	50,958,643
18	Hong Kong (HKG)	50,410,819
19	Madrid (MAD)	49,786,202
20	Houston (IAH, HOU)	49,533,570

Source: Airports Council International, 2010.

STAY CLOSE

The light-rail Hiawatha Line in the Twin Cities, anchored by a stadium on one end and destination retail on the other, has attracted the development of more than 15,000 residential units in its first years of operation.

global marketplace, the importance of these gateways is enhanced by direct connections through expansive international airports, high-speed rail, well-managed freeways, and next-generation communications infrastructure.

GATEWAY PREMIUMS

The world's gateway cities and their surrounding megaregions will continue to attract and concentrate wealth, whether in exclusive condominium residences with stratospheric price tags or in massive commercial-district skyscrapers. They have become expensive safe havens for capital preservation with opportunities for value creation well beyond those of secondary and tertiary locations. London, Tokyo, New York, Hong Kong, and Paris will continue to command these significant premiums, as will many other financial hubs connected on international flight paths, such as São Paulo, Shanghai, Toronto, San Francisco, Los Angeles, Houston, and Washington, D.C. Is it any surprise that the condominium market in Miami, a gateway fueled by its direct connections to Latin America, rebounded from the housing crash ahead of other parts of Florida? Or that Chicago has withstood regional economic decline better than other Midwest cities? It shouldn't be. Regional centers—like Atlanta, Istanbul, Moscow, and Frankfurt—also gain from their important airport hubs. In fact, any place with a strategic airport or port garners a competitive edge. It's about access and volume.

LOCAL MOTION

A new wave of local infrastructure leadership is repositioning communities and regions for the better. Communities are implementing new mobility frameworks to meet competition on the global stage, and by doing so they are enhancing the quality of life for residents in unexpected ways.

Focus on:

NORTH TEXAS'S AEROPOLIS Alliance Airport, owned by the city of Fort Worth, is the anchor for the nation's fastest-growing industrial hub. Repeatedly cited as the top foreign trade zone in the United States, it is connected to two rail carriers and is being upgraded to expand runways. With immediate proximity to the world's eighth busiest airport, Dallas–Fort Worth International (DFW), North Texas is a logistics powerhouse. Not content to stand still, DFW is being upgraded in a public/private strategy that connects passenger rail to the airport in an information-driven manner that connects to the city's hospitality and retail venues and provides seamless mobility from ground to air.

Biking in Copenhagen.

COPENHAGEN'S BICYCLE SUPERPATH The Danish capital's 500-kilometer bicycle network is expanding to become a regional super-network.

KUALA LUMPUR RAIL With the world's second-highest number of cars per capita, the city has set annual targets to increase the modal share of transit.

HOUSTON TRANSIT Yes, Houston. The city will grow its light-rail network to 69 stations over 38.9 miles of track by 2014, opening new opportunities for mixed-use development.

Accessibility also works its magic within the premier "24-hour" cities and their suburbs, which tend to feature the world's best urban infrastructure bones—subways, buses, and light rail branching through pedestrian-friendly business centers and walkable neighborhoods and linking to airports and increasingly, regional high-speed rail service. People can move about and get things done despite chronically congested roads. This access adds value.

CENTERING

Convenience plays into the desires of many in the now emerging gen-Y demographic, too. More connected to each other than any previous generation, these young adults crave the interaction that is possible in central gathering places around stimulating environs. Texting facilitates instantaneous meeting, and social networking keeps friends apprised of current activities. Delaying marriage and kids, gen-Yers put up with cramped living quarters to gain the benefits of short commutes and nearby nightlife, entertainment venues, and parks. For many, affordable mass transit beats the hassle and expense of owning a car (not just loan payments, insurance, repairs, gas, but also parking). Others rent when they need to drive, using shared cars.

UNDERLYING VALUE

On a more granular level, accessibility and mobility networks drive real estate decision making within metropolitan areas. Homes near transit stations command a growing premium. So does convenient access to stores, schools, and parks. Homebuyers and renters recognize how paying more makes sense for those locations that reduce the costs and time they spend moving about. As strapped communities struggle with the costs of maintaining transit networks, they embrace less expensive mass transit solutions—light rail and bus rapid transit—which are connected to legacy systems. More and more local businesses and residents support these initiatives in voter referendums, despite general anti-spending sentiment.

QUICK VERSUS FAR

Neighborhoods that connect most directly and easily to urban nodes and downtown centers will gain advantages over less convenient (exurban) locations. Three-hour daily commutes through stop-and-go traffic look less appealing when compared with half-hour drives or mass transit connections. The tradeoff becomes more compelling against the backdrop of cratered housing values in outer suburbs. And when gen-Y leaves the cities to raise families or seek suburban lifestyles, these more-convenient suburbs likely will be tops on their house-hunting lists.

INTEGRATED OVER ISOLATED

As a result, the target sites for developers and homebuilders shift over the next generation from the fringe to infill, with an emphasis on creating greater convenience in attractive communities. "Smart" planning looks to integrate rather than separate commercial, residential, and recreational uses. The models need not break new ground—they can emulate examples of the leading international gateways or, on a smaller scale, the traditional main street–centered village.

> "Regional cooperation is the foundation of sound policy and is absolutely necessary for sustainable growth. To maintain our economic competitive advantage and quality of life, we must develop regional solutions to the critical issues facing our states."
>
> **JEB BUSH,**
> FORMER GOVERNOR OF FLORIDA, AT 2012 ULI FLORIDA SUMMIT IN TAMPA, FLORIDA

TOP WORLD UNIVERSITIES

Rank	University	City
1	University of Cambridge	Cambridge, UK
2	Harvard University	Cambridge, MA
3	Massachusetts Institute of Technology	Cambridge, MA
4	Yale University	New Haven, CT
5	University of Oxford	Oxford, UK
6	Imperial College London	London, UK
7	University College London	London, UK
8	University of Chicago	Chicago, IL
9	University of Pennsylvania	Philadelphia, PA
10	Columbia University	New York City, NY
11	Stanford University	Stanford, CA
12	California Institute of Technology	Pasadena, CA
13	Princeton University	Princeton, NJ
14	University of Michigan	Ann Arbor, MI
15	Cornell University	Ithaca, NY
16	Johns Hopkins University	Baltimore, MD
17	McGill University	Montreal, Canada
18	ETH Zürich—Swiss Federal Institute of Technology Zürich	Zurich, Switzerland
19	Duke University	Durham, NC
20	University of Edinburgh	Edinburgh, UK

Source: *U.S. News and World Report* (2011).
Note: *U.S. News and World Report* rankings are based on data from the QS World University Rankings, which are produced in association with QS Quacquarelli Symonds. The rankings are based on such factors as academic reputation, faculty, employer reputation, and faculty/student ratio, among others.

Inviting public space takes greater precedence over private space as the suburban disconnection pursued so eagerly in the recent past—the subdivision house-and-yard concept—has lost some of its attraction. Infill multifamily development will more likely include retail components, and planners will move to embrace concepts that create appealing streetscapes with commercial life that encourages pedestrian activity. Lively places are more enticing, interesting, and friendly, especially for the gen-Y cohort, which developers want to attract. Legacy institutions within cities become a fundamental building block for rebuilding communities that were once left behind by inward-facing campus plans.

The United States, with more than half the world's leading educational institutions, sees the impacts associated with land use decisions by these local universities extend far beyond surrounding neighborhoods.

REAL SOCIAL NETWORKS

Aging baby boomers want greater convenience too. More-urban environments make it easier to get to nearby stores or cultural attractions, often on foot. And an aging population group facing more medical hiccups generally finds readier access to doctors and hospitals in 24-hour markets. Downsizing 60-somethings will gravitate

Koreatown Galleria in Los Angeles.

NEWCOMERS PHONE HOME

Immigrant neighborhoods have become important assets to all cities. Not only do these communities serve as bastions of diversity and drivers of local economies, they also deliver local links to global communities in rapidly growing emerging markets.

Focus on:

KOREATOWN The Wilshire Center Koreatown neighborhood in Los Angeles is home to a patchwork of cultures and ethnicities that have become a nexus for global investment in the city. Coordinated public and private actions have resulted in high-density zoning, production of workforce housing, transit improvements, a business improvement district, special design guidelines, and billions of dollars of ongoing investment during the recent downturn. Whether Korean, Mexican, Guatemalan, or Salvadoran, neighborhood-based businesses and institutions form a direct conduit for foreign capital into Los Angeles and a lively network back to origin markets.

FLUSHING Located in New York City's Queens at the terminus of the famed No. 7 subway line, this community is now the second largest Chinatown in the world. With direct access to regional rail, highways, and two airports, this neighborhood sports vitality and global access.

WILHELMSBURG Across the river from downtown Hamburg, this diverse neighborhood is anchored by new Balkan immigrants. The city's IBA Hamburg project is empowering the neighborhood through business incubation, new schools, and stakeholder-driven experiments in new workforce housing.

to more amply sized apartments and townhouses than their gen-Y offspring. They do not necessarily want to forsake spacious rooms, they just want fewer of them to take care of.

LINKED IN BY REGION

For secondary and tertiary markets, the prospects for economic growth will improve through augmented connections to the nearest gateway cities and their transport hubs. Infrastructure improvements can become competitive game changers for some places. China has turbocharged its recent economic growth with regional high-speed rail connections integrated into extensive urban subway systems and linked to airports. Advanced high-speed train networks in Europe, Japan, and Korea have benefited regional economic activity, enhancing travel between business centers. In the United States, which lags in passenger rail capacity, deficit concerns limit appetites for the necessary government outlays to build new systems, sidelining proposed, large-price-tag, high-speed rail projects.

The country could gain by concentrating resources in high-density urban corridors like the Northeast megaregion between Washington, D.C., and Boston and connecting high-population cities in California. Many sprawling Sunbelt metropolitan areas—developed around roads and interstate highways—will attempt to implement light-rail expansions and bus rapid transit systems to relieve clogged highways and reestablish center city hubs, if government budget shortfalls do not stand in the way. Developers will continue to seek opportunities for residential and mixed-use projects near stations along mass transit routes.

>> **IN A MORE CROWDED AND INTERCONNECTED WORLD, THE ABILITY TO AVOID HASSLES ADDS MORE VALUE, AND CONVENIENCE BECOMES EVER MORE PRIZED.**

"How do we design cities without eight-lane arterials and without superblocks?"

PETER CALTHORPE,
2006 ULI NICHOLS PRIZE WINNER AND PRESIDENT, CALTHORPE ASSOCIATES, AT 2012 PAN ASIA DEVELOPMENT CONFERENCE IN BEIJING, CHINA

MAKE OVER

HOW WILL YOU **REINVENT** YOUR

SPACE?

MAKE OVER

HOW WILL YOU **REINVENT, RECAPITALIZE,** AND **REPOSITION** YOUR EXISTING ASSETS?

ADAPT, REDO, MAKE OVER, and think again—that has always been a part of the real estate credo for success. For more than a generation, real estate minds have worked on central cities as places needing reinvention. The exodus to the suburbs suggested that the urban experience had passed its prime, but although the work is never done, countless downtowns have now been turned around and mixed-use vitality has been restored.

BACK TO THE "BURBS"

Well, time to rethink again. As revitalization strategies push out from the urban core, we see the bloom of many suburban neighborhoods has faded. Poor planning legacies and low-quality execution are now joined by new waves of demographics and a dose of lifestyle obsolescence. Commodity developments age poorly, old malls continue to die, office parks lose value, and uncontrollable congestion restricts mobility. Problems once confined to "cities"—poverty, crime, underperforming schools, budget deficits, failing infrastructure, and tax base erosion—have spread across metropolitan areas and seeped into many suburban districts. Since the foreclosure crisis, the race to the suburbs appears stalled, or at least poised for reinvention. Around the world, existing suburbs represent a new frontier.

Solutions defy the simplicity of single-jurisdiction efforts and historic or cultural restoration strategies deployed in city centers. The suburban reinvention proposition typically involves competing jurisdictions and planning staffs inexperienced with rethinking old rules. Elected officials grapple with transforming ghost malls and unfinished residential subdivisions. New strategies include relocating city halls and churches, clearing the way for parks or, for the lucky few who have transit funding, new streetcars or bus rapid transit lines. In stronger markets, private initiatives explore creating ambitious new town centers by reworking parking and introducing residential uses into commercial zones. At the exurban edge, reworking suburbs may mean reversing course, with land acquired for subdivisions reverting to agriculture. Farmers are looking pretty smart as they buy back land low that they sold high ten years ago.

> "Do not think of achieving benefits from one cost. Think of costs as profit centers to be maximized. Think of energy efficiency as a convenient vehicle to unlock many doors to sources of value."
>
> **AMORY LOVINS,**
> CHAIRMAN, ROCKY MOUNTAIN INSTITUTE, AT 2012 ULI SPRING MEETING IN CHARLOTTE, NORTH CAROLINA

SUBURBAN CENTERS

Once-disparaged suburban strip corridors are being transformed into mixed-use neighborhoods through coordinated leadership, new land use visions, and implementation partnerships. The results: vibrant, mixed-use communities that function as retail destinations as well as the location of community amenities and new formats for residential living.

Focus on:

NEW WHITE FLINT Rockville Pike in Montgomery County in Maryland has been known as the Washington, D.C. metropolitan region's most congested suburban strip, a place where it is nearly impossible to walk. Originally designed for the car, the corridor's anchor was the White Flint Mall—surrounded by parking lots. In less than three years, the new White Flint Partnership—a consortium of competing landowners—is implementing a coordinated vision to create a vibrant, walkable commercial and residential corridor.

BELLEVUE Once the sprawling suburb of Seattle, Washington, Bellevue is now attracting blue-chip corporations to its new transit-oriented downtown. Will this former bedroom community upstage Tacoma as Seattle's "twin" city?

VIENNA The Austrian capital's tired Südbahnhof is being transformed into a new Central Station that extends well beyond new rail infrastructure. A new "city within the suburbs," the project delivers office space for 20,000 new jobs, 5,000 apartments, and a new university campus.

Pike & Rose is a planned mixed-use neighborhood that will provide shopping, entertainment, and residential space in the White Flint district in Rockville, Maryland.

UNFINISHED BUSINESS IN THE CORE

Despite a rebound in select major markets, the urban regeneration agenda will continue to need care and feeding. Cities that stand still or put their urban core on ice risk falling farther behind one of the most overwhelming and unprecedented trends in communities around the world. Both large and small cities reinvent old manufacturing sites into entertainment districts like Denver's LoDo or funky high-tech districts like @22 Barcelona. And then there are the Detroits, where reinvention is a marathon involving tough choices to rewrite the city's DNA. Gentrification will continue in markets where ambitious residents can afford to vote with their feet—rowhouses to townhouses, rotting piers to art parks, abandoned factories to lofts cum trattorias and brownfields into bike paths and restored habitat. Adjacent properties reap the benefits of higher values created by new community amenities and the influx of demographic cohorts creating new urban markets.

HOUSING: TEN LEAST AFFORDABLE U.S. CITIES

HOI[a]	Metro area	AMI[b]
1	New York, NY	$81,300
2	San Francisco, CA	$96,700
3	Bridgeport, CT	$106,700
4	Ocean City, NJ	$71,100
5	Santa Ana, CA	$70,100
6	Los Angeles, CA	$70,100
7	San Jose, CA	$105,000
8	San Luis Obispo, CA	$75,400
9	Honolulu, HI	$82,700
10	Santa Cruz, CA	$87,000

Sources: National Association of Home Builders/Wells Fargo report; Fannie Mae/Federal Housing Finance Agency, 2012–2013.
Note: Data for second quarter of 2012.
[a] Housing opportunity index.
[b] HUD area median income.

PRESERVING HOUSING CHOICES

But as neighborhood revitalization continues to benefit communities as a whole, it is always accompanied by challenges. As existing lower-income residents seek opportunity, community leaders will have to forge new partnerships to deliver the housing products they want and need. The recent profit play in multifamily development markets has focused predictably on more affluent segments. As the cost to construct new housing pencils out at rents most people cannot pay, private and nonprofit investors will look at creative solutions involving mixing incomes and harnessing the aggregation of foreclosed single-family housing stock. Local governments will have to become entrepreneurial partners in order to identify new solutions—like converting closed public school buildings into public housing or helping to transform vacant office buildings into apartments on the scale that Philadelphia has accomplished over the last decade.

SNEAKING INTO THE BOX

Rethinking and repurposing obsolescent buildings builds momentum in the private sector too. Ambitious buyers with insight into capturing new markets can acquire underused assets on the cheap in today's

> "One square yard of Texas prairie supports hundreds of plant, insect, and bacteria species. That is exactly how community resilience should be approached—not by an obvious 'hardening' and dehumanizing of buildings, but by designing them to be flexible and adaptable when put under stress."
>
> **RIVES TAYLOR,**
> DIRECTOR OF SUSTAINABLE DESIGN, GENSLER

The boardwalk along Toronto's Lake Ontario waterfront not only uses a playful, natural shape, but also attracts visitors with different walkway levels and amenities such as slides for children.

WATERFRONT REDO

The redevelopment of urban waterfronts was "discovered" in the 1990s as environmental risk was mitigated on brownfields sites. Today, a new round of major projects moves forward with a heightened awareness of the need to build self-sustaining mixed-use neighborhoods that provide unique public value to regional stakeholders.

Focus on:

TORONTO The reworking of Toronto's Lake Ontario waterfront is, at 800 hectares, one of North America's largest urban redevelopment initiatives. With Canadian immigration policies supplying a steady stream of apartment buyers and renters, annual absorption has been steady at over 15,000 units per year. New critical mass is being achieved through greater transit access, a new campus for George Brown College, an athletes village for the 2014 Pan-American Games, and innovative public spaces that redefine urban living.

BROOKLYN Mayor Bloomberg's initiative to reposition sites along the East River is bearing fruit in the form of new parks and new private mixed-use projects.

HONG KONG Hong Kong's world-class brand is getting a world-class waterfront, after the city asked a ULI Advisory Panel to appropriately balance stakeholder interests in the redevelopment of Kai Tak airport.

ALEXANDRIA This historic town in Virginia kicked off the waterfront "makeover" theme 30 years ago and is in the midst of defining new strategies to spur a greater mixture of urban uses.

slumbering markets. A hula-hoop factory becomes a film production studio in Newark. A lumberyard is refashioned with authentic wood finishes into upscale retail in Malibu. A left-for-dead department store is converted to a university in Chicago. And a textile mill turns into a music center in Charlotte. Meanwhile, an Ottoman-era train station is now an arts-oriented retail center in Tel Aviv and a modernist Class C office building is the hippest hotel in Vienna. And the list goes on—every city has its own extraordinary examples.

A $1 million renovation turned a former gas station on 11th Street in Long Island City into the Breadbox Café.

JUST VISITING

At another extreme, proposing new uses in the "sharing economy" may mean delivering services, not product. Virtual office providers from Jakarta to Berlin to Kansas City let small start-up companies gain the prestige of commercial-district office locations without the expense of renting permanent space. Online reservation systems allow use of space to be managed and extended. "Tenants" pay service companies for a club-like opportunity to spin the fiction of a strategic address to place on letterhead and websites, remote receptionist and other business support services, a snail mail drop, and office bays or conference rooms for occasional meetings. A spare room and a sofa now becomes a bed and breakfast and a new revenue stream. Is it a hotel, café, incubator, night school, or call center? New uses in existing buildings transform as people work from any hotspot. Established corporations leverage shared incubators as their employees seek to stay productive while travelling from city to city.

TRIED AND TRUE VALUE

Reworking real estate will always include the good old form of aggressive asset management, where the dusting and buffing of landscapes, finishes, and lobbies have now been joined by

> "A virtual blizzard of sustainability metrics has emerged over the past few years. From an investment manager's perspective, we need standardized metrics to measure both financial and operating performance of buildings."
>
> **PATRICIA CONNOLLY,**
> GLOBAL DIRECTOR OF SUSTAINABILITY, RREEF, AND COCHAIR, ULI NEW YORK SUSTAINABILITY COMMITTEE, AT 2012 ULI SPRING MEETING IN CHARLOTTE, NORTH CAROLINA

comprehensive energy demand management. Many cash-flow-starved, underwater borrowers have delayed improvements to buildings, either waiting for recapitalization or leaving the hard work to the next owner following a foreclosure or squeeze-out. Deft operators may be able to shift resources from operating budgets to help pay for capital investments, which enable successful lease-up strategies, tenant retention, and maybe increased rents. Owners in receptive jurisdictions may be able to call their utility or city energy office and seize retrofit subsidies or gain access to a tranche of low-interest debt. Voila—restored operating budgets.

WORKING OUT

Pulled by the undertow of economic uncertainty, owners must continuously rework finances to climb out from an extremely deep debt hole, each property part of a refinance slog of more than $1 trillion in maturing mortgages in the United States alone. Those asset-by-asset workouts will come in waves in the near term and continue to dribble out over the course of the decade. This baseline of refinance activity will cumulatively shape the profile of this decade's best professional practices in asset management.

MAKING SAUSAGE

Overhauling the real estate industry's financial rules will be a mandatory component of the decade's workout routine, and it may end up being the legacy event. The spate of commercial real estate busts raises the question of whether property markets offer enough

HOW OWNERS ARE ACHIEVING ENERGY EFFICIENCY

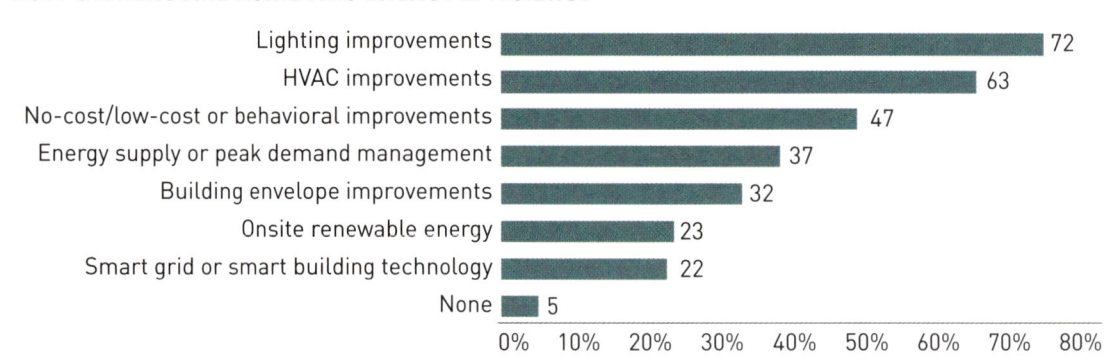

Category	%
Lighting improvements	72
HVAC improvements	63
No-cost/low-cost or behavioral improvements	47
Energy supply or peak demand management	37
Building envelope improvements	32
Onsite renewable energy	23
Smart grid or smart building technology	22
None	5

Source: Institute for Building Efficiency/ULI Energy Efficiency Indicators Survey, 2011.

investment-grade products to satisfy the potential levels of global capital flows. Investors always find trouble when analysis is cut short, buildings are packaged as commodities, and profits are justified by transaction binges. Buying and flipping works when demand allows; it fails miserably as a sole long-term strategy. When investment managers promise outsized performance, caveat emptor: real estate has trouble delivering consistent opportunistic returns.

The REIT universe has had more success in managing volatility by cornering much of the best product in select asset sectors and global gateways. These properties tend to perform better through ups and downs, and can sustain high valuations. But differentiated tenant demand for second- and third-tier real estate products requires a wider risk spread, an understanding of local tenants, and underlying relationships to keep buildings leased up. Driving down capitalization rates on commodity properties never ends well.

The Hudson Yards project on the west side of Manhattan is connecting to the High Line elevated park and the No. 7 line subway, which extends east into Queens. The 12 million-square-foot master-planned project recycles long-underused land into a medley of public and private uses that fundamentally reposition the neighborhood.

>> **MAKING OVER AND WORKING OUT MAY AVOID REPETITION OF PAST MISTAKES.**

JUMP AHEAD

ARE YOU READY TO **ADAPT**?

©SANDY HUFFAKER/CORBIS

JUMP AHEAD

WHAT IS THE **VALUE** OF YOUR ASSET IN THE "AGE OF CLICKS"?

HOW WILL **DEMOGRAPHICS** SHIFT MARKET PREFERENCES?

IS **ATTENTION TO LOCATION** THE "SMARTEST" DECISION OF ALL?

MEETING FUTURE MARKET CONDITIONS REQUIRES STRATEGIC THINKING AND ANTICIPATION. LEADERSHIP IS BEING THERE TO SERVE BEFORE BEING ASKED.

STEPPING OUT OF SEQUENCE

At the center of market dislocations stands real estate. The assumptions and expectations for where and how we live and work will continue to evolve in the context of the aftermath of the housing market collapse and a skittish recovery in credit markets, against the baseline of technological reinvention and demographic change. Buoying the industry in Asia and South America are expanding middle classes seeking to make choices and vote with their wallets. But North American real estate markets should benefit from population gains, too, with immigration and natural growth augmenting demand for space in the coming decade and beyond. In contrast, Japan and most major European markets, including Italy and Germany, face the prospect of ebbing populations and contraction in some real estate markets.

TIMING THE LONG TERM

Leaders in real estate should seize emerging opportunities dictated by the new realities—making good out of bad. As the industry stays lean and works harder—and differently—to boost profits, its entrepreneurial premiums and resilience will get put to the test. What worked in the past or even last year may not work again. The cost and complexity of projects increase while the market's willingness or ability to pay may decline along with investment returns. The one-size-fits-all approach no longer reigns: markets within property sectors fragment into ever more niches. Understanding and anticipating new tenant needs becomes crucial to success as decision making becomes more opaque, at times influenced as much by global forces as by local market quirks.

INTERNALIZING TECHNOLOGY

Effective use of technology enables easy urban navigation, more efficient use of space, and building-performance monitoring. For expense-conscious tenants, new applications of technology can translate into smart use of every square foot and a new market push

> "Each cycle is different. You won't see it coming and you won't know the depth or duration. You must operate your business with that knowledge. It will affect your ability to access capital and it will affect demand. I learned this time that ... while you seem to have alignment with [your investor partners] on the up cycle, you may not on the down cycle."
>
> **RON TERWILLIGER,**
> CHAIRMAN, ULI TERWILLIGER CENTER FOR HOUSING, AND CHAIRMAN EMERITUS, TRAMMELL CROW RESIDENTIAL

to force developers, architects, landlords, and investors to acknowledge technology's disruption of everything. And although accessible location remains the key variable influencing real estate value, information technology is changing retail formats, transforming interior space design, opening global markets for professional services, and fundamentally blurring the distinction between office and home. A world of handheld information means we can do more from just about anywhere. Operating from a particular place in a specific space is no longer as critical. Advantage goes to those smart enough to embrace technology's reach into new pools of value.

BROWN TO GREEN

For office buildings, the story starts with cost reductions but ends with gen-Y and workforce productivity. Better light and healthier air make working more pleasant, reduce sick days, and attract a new generation of knowledge workers. Then consider how cloud computing is reducing the need for on-site server space. Digitalization means law firms might ditch libraries. Young, vanguard workers demand cutting-edge, environmentally friendly buildings, so the human resources department may be driving tenants' real estate decisions. No office developer should forsake this kind of green, nor should investors buy brown without discounting the competitive consequences and retrofitting costs. The expense of transforming brown to green must be part of any acquisition equation. That's just being smart.

HOW OWNERS ARE MANAGING PROJECT COSTS

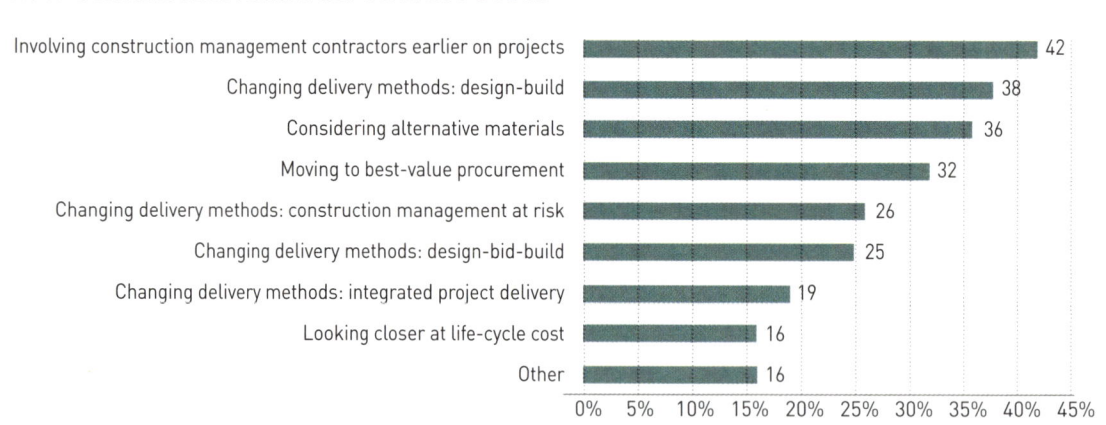

Involving construction management contractors earlier on projects	42
Changing delivery methods: design-build	38
Considering alternative materials	36
Moving to best-value procurement	32
Changing delivery methods: construction management at risk	26
Changing delivery methods: design-bid-build	25
Changing delivery methods: integrated project delivery	19
Looking closer at life-cycle cost	16
Other	16

Source: Institute for Building Efficiency/JCI ULI EEI Survey, 2011.

ENERGY FUTURES

Communities are using technology, incentives, and new regulations to transform their markets to embrace the value of energy efficiency, market transparency, and building retrofits. By transforming the energy performance of their existing building stock, these cities are working toward goals of net zero buildings.

Focus on:

SINGAPORE Having reduced energy use intensity by 15 percent since 1990 and carbon intensity by 25 percent, Singapore has a suite of incentives, low-interest loans, and new reporting requirements. Finance mechanisms have been introduced to allow accelerated one-year depreciation of new technologies in commercial buildings, as well as an aggressive multifamily "en bloc" strategy that rewards residents for participating in vast modernization and building retrofit programs.

AUSTIN Leveraging its municipally owned utility, this Texas city is the first in the United States to require energy use disclosure at time of sale.

The National Library in Singapore.

LONDON The city's Better Buildings Partnership is a consortium of owners reducing their carbon footprint by 60 percent by 2025. It has partnered with the ULI Greenprint Center for Building Performance.

NEW YORK Mayor Bloomberg's Greener, Greater Buildings initiative is generating unprecedented data on how buildings consume energy in the city.

MOVING TECHNOLOGY

Yet a plethora of green technologies remains untapped. True, more solar arrays on expansive mall and warehouse rooftops are producing revenue streams, but only in jurisdictions with aggressive incentive programs. New controls and dimmers, new glazing systems, and the lightbulb wars create uncertainty and keep high-tech out of projects. At least for the moment. Capturing value may involve doing more than checking boxes. It may require working with tenants, the city, the state, or even the utility to create cost-benefit structures that move new technologies into old buildings.

HOME WORK

The delivery of smart homes has room to grow, too. Carving out space for a home office enables professionals to roll out of bed and get on that conference call. Delivering appropriately wired homes

JUMP AHEAD

ANTICIPATED CHANGE IN CLEANTECH SPENDING AMONG WORLD'S LARGEST CORPORATIONS (2012–2014)

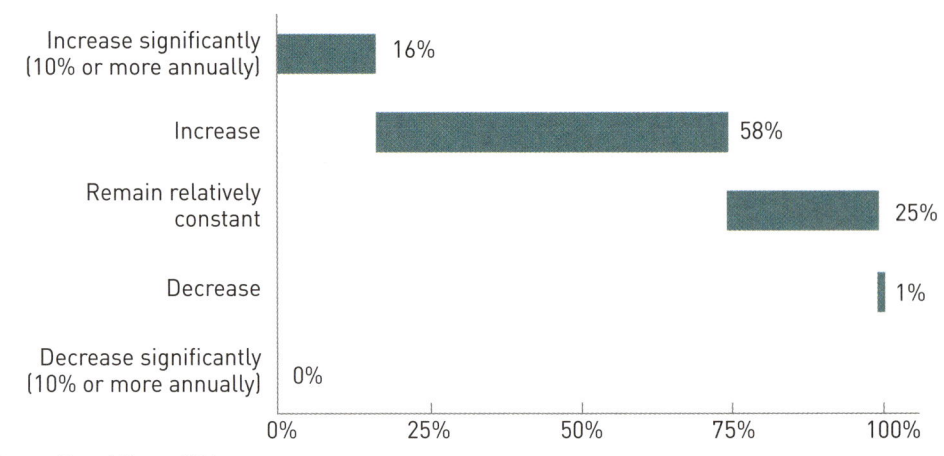

Category	Percentage
Increase significantly (10% or more annually)	16%
Increase	58%
Remain relatively constant	25%
Decrease	1%
Decrease significantly (10% or more annually)	0%

Source: Ernst & Young, 2011.
Note: Cleantech is defined by Ernst & Young as "the umbrella term for the range of technologies, goods, and services that minimize or eliminate the environmental impact of economic activity and form the basis of the corporate response to climate change."

provides a perk all buyers want. Remotely managing energy systems, HVAC, and security are features some may even pay more for. For apartment dwellers, functional home offices may not require an additional room. Gen-Y renters, who nourish themselves on social networking, will look to common spaces for tech amenities in buildings.

DELIVERING THE VANGUARD

As the new home market firms up, expect more homebuilders to get on the smart-home bandwagon. KB Homes is delivering a net-zero energy home that reduces electricity bills nearly to nothing. When prospective buyers realize that savings add up to an estimated $6,000 annually, more will start to pay attention and do the math. The designs are smart to the extent that the homes represent a package of integrated technologies including efficient building envelopes, lighting, appliances, fixtures, and solar panels—and the control systems to pull it all together in a consumer-friendly fashion.

RETAIL MAKEOVERS

Touch-and-feel retail experiences become less necessary when buyers save time and gas money by buying online. Even skeptics have come to their senses and acknowledge how internet shopping will continue to erode bricks-and-mortar market shares. At

> "The notion of homeownership as the American dream can no longer be taken as a grand truth."
>
> **GEORGE CASEY,**
> CEO, ORLEANS HOMEBUILDERS, AT 2012 ULI FLORIDA SUMMIT IN TAMPA, FLORIDA

a minimum, major chains are incorporating mobile applications and web connections to help ensure sales growth. From apparel to electronics, retailers are reducing in-store selections, focusing on what shoppers really want and need, and offering greater variety on integrated websites with delivery at home. Banks are shrinking their networks as customers gravitate to online payments and deposits, and eventually mobile wallets. And we know what happened to booksellers and record stores—poof.

Retailers are moving to cut operating costs. Best Buy and Bose have set up vending machines and kiosks at airports. Kohl's and Walmart are moving on solar roofs. Target, Home Depot, and the Container Store are opening stores with urban formats. These stores merge online and in-store ordering and purchasing opportunities. Many of these are multistory and mixed-use formats resulting from new public/private partnerships that tackle thorny issues like parking and access.

This will be the decade when we find out who will live above a Walmart—in this case, a proposed mixed-use, adaptive-use project in Washington, D.C. that rewrites the rules for retail formats.

ONLINE RETAIL SALES, 2009–2014 AND 2020 ($ BILLIONS)

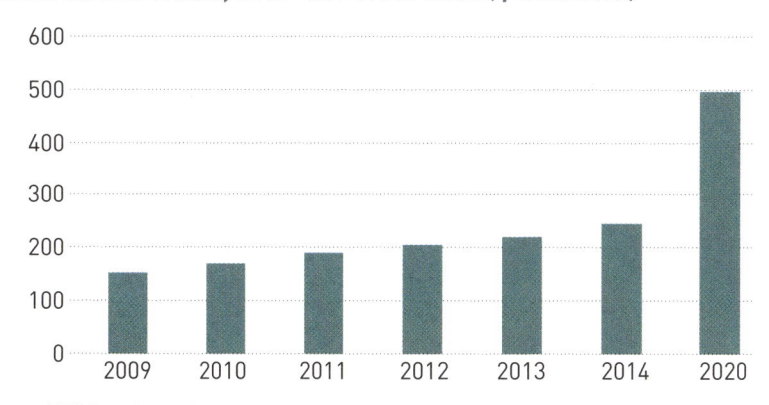

Sources: NRF Foundation; Forrester Research; IBM; NYU Stern School of Business.
Note: Online retail sales is defined as purchasing items via a web transaction.

WHAT'S NEXT? GETTING AHEAD OF CHANGE 53

THE REALITY OF VIRTUAL

Social websites can be a boon if harnessed properly. They feature apps for product ratings and reviews with advertising links to stores and shopper wish lists to help draw customer traffic and enhance visits. Owners of destination retail rely increasingly on entertainment and food to draw consumers; they are adopting the internet as another distribution channel to boost in-line store sales. On entering malls or retail districts, shoppers receive sales tips, information about store openings, and special offers. They can locate specific stores or merchandise, receive special discounts, and save time otherwise spent on hunting for what they want.

It can all add up to much more enjoyment and surprise. Big owners can further their advantage over weaker competitors who cannot execute integrated strategies. Interactive information systems can also be installed in sidewalks for urban shopping districts. Madrid's recent "iPavement" pilot project, providing wi-fi and local information to passers-by, pioneers this technology. In a time-constrained world, a smart retailing experience with new options, decisions, and conveniences beats the old-school mall crawl any day.

iREALESTATE

Web-enabled services prove a blessing to smaller real estate players, who can operate with lower overhead while partnering and collaborating from disparate sites through instant communications and information sharing. From mapping apps to online data providers that give instant access to wide-ranging market intelligence, even the smallest real estate shops can assess the same opportunities as the big guys.

LOGISTICS

For manufacturers and shippers, more web-based selling and tracking means that logistics models will drive ongoing change, reducing needs for storage space and increasing demand for specialized distribution facilities to move orders quickly to buyers. Industrial developers will gain ground in constructing build-to-suit complexes that enable speedy point-to-point fulfillment. Pick-and-pack operations may require better air conditioning and more parking than typical warehouse distribution space.

> "The internet will massively disrupt the education and utility industries over the course of this decade."
>
> **STEVE CASE,**
> CHAIRMAN AND CEO, REVOLUTION, AT ULI'S HONOR AWARD CEREMONY AT THE NATIONAL BUILDING MUSEUM

Lake Nona, outside Orlando, Florida, is a fast-growing, innovative master-planned community. Encompassing 7,000 acres, four major medical facilities, housing, and retail space, Lake Nona is expected to employ more than 30,000 people and have an economic impact of $8 billion.

MONITORING PERFORMANCE

Whether working at a project site or in multiple office locations, architects, engineers, and builders can monitor design-build projects and simultaneously control costs. Building managers can keep closer tabs on systems to spot inefficiencies and reduce loads in real time. Brokers can reach tenant prospects or potential buyers with tailored information to enhance deal prospects. Many of their targets will be technology companies—the fastest-growing sector in the economy—that would expect nothing less.

INNOVATION OCCUPIES BUILDINGS

It follows that smart investment bets will pursue opportunities where tech industries tend to concentrate. Local officials can promote jobs and tax base growth off smart technology, too. Lake Nona, Orlando's fastest-growing master-planned community, booms around a health and life sciences cluster of hospitals, research institutions, and research companies.

South Lake Union, Seattle.

DEVELOPING LOCAL INNOVATION

Joining San Francisco, Boston, and San Diego, more cities are using universities as tools to promote business innovation and incubation to attract new industries, create jobs, and develop a competition-ready workforce. By creating strong partnerships and new intermediaries, cities employing high-quality, place-based development strategies are reinforcing economic development frameworks rooted in the innovation economy.

Focus on:

SEATTLE The transition from a company-based to a university-based economic development strategy is underway. Fourteen education and medical centers provide over 15 percent of the jobs. The University of Washington has launched a commercialization initiative and a business incubator called C4C New Ventures Facility, to double the number of startups produced in the city over the next three years. Major place-based developments, including South Lake Union, are catering to new economic sectors fueled by primary research in life sciences and information technologies.

BEIJING Over 70 universities, including China's elite Tsinghua and Beijing universities, have attracted hundreds of global corporations, now agglomerated in the city's northwest quadrant. Foreign universities have followed suit, setting up shop to attract China's best and brightest.

NEW YORK In a dramatic attempt to recruit technology companies to New York, the city selected Cornell University to redevelop long-vacant Roosevelt Island. A second consortium is to take on the Brooklyn Navy Yard.

DISRUPTIVE LEARNING

The business of making people smarter is evolving in the face of skyrocketing tuitions, parents' dwindling college savings accounts, the student loan crisis, and strained university budgets. Leading universities seek to tap lower-cost, potentially high-revenue-generating opportunities in online education and distance learning. They can get a greater bang for the buck out of their prestigious brands, potentially reaching more students without providing high-cost campus services or expanding facilities. Online students may lose the campus experience and direct interaction with professors, but they earn degrees without incurring as much debt. And what will this mean for markets dependent on colleges and universities? The smart players should take notice—demand for student housing could come off the boil at some schools, while universities may require specialized studios and tech support to expand their reach or establish regional service centers to house student get-togethers or provide tutoring.

A globally issued request for proposals and the promise of a contribution of land combined to attract Cornell University and the Technion-Israel Institute of Technology to Roosevelt Island in New York City's East River.

>> **VALUING THE FLOW OF INFORMATION THROUGH BUILDINGS AND PLACES IS ONLY SMART.**

WHAT'S NEXT? GETTING AHEAD OF CHANGE

KEEP WATCH

ARE YOUR EYES OPEN TO WHAT LIES

AHEAD?

KEEP WATCH

ARE YOUR **EYES OPEN** TO WHAT LIES AHEAD?

DO YOU HAVE YOUR **EARS TO THE GROUND**—EVERYWHERE?

UNCERTAINTY. UNCERTAINTY. UNCERTAINTY. There's so much uncertainty we're almost uncertain about what to be uncertain about. Where is the world headed? It seems more topsy-turvy than ever—or does it?

Officials wrestle with ongoing financial market disruption. Europe looks bad. How stable is China? Energy prices continue to ratchet up and down. What do new regulations—Basel III, Dodd-Frank—mean for real estate? What do we do about entitlement overload and overly complicated, loophole-filled tax codes? The traditional family is no longer the norm. And then there are the inevitable bolts out of the blue—natural disasters, regional conflicts, and climate impacts. They seem to undermine confidence more than they might in less unstable times.

Information comes at us faster and in greater volumes than ever, but it can be harder to process and analyze. You almost always can find data or commentary that makes your case, but how accurate is it, can you fool yourself, and could you be misleading your clients and partners? Increased transparency does not necessarily bring greater clarity or an appropriate context.

REALITY CHECKED

Under the circumstances, it pays to have your wits about you, be alert, and stay aware. It's certainly no time to relax, and probably a

ULI DISTRICT COUNCIL SURVEY
What is the greatest challenge to growth and development in your region?

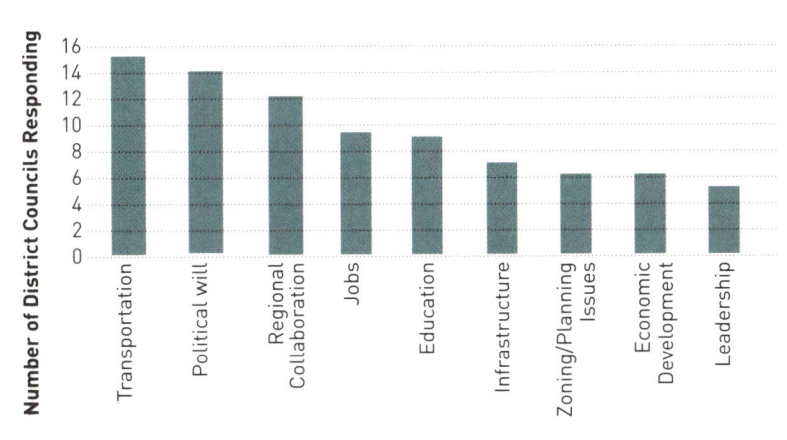

Category	Number of District Councils Responding
Transportation	15
Political will	14
Regional Collaboration	12
Jobs	9
Education	9
Infrastructure	7
Zoning/Planning Issues	6
Economic Development	6
Leadership	5

Source: ULI survey of District Councils, summer 2012.

> "Our generation has got to stop kicking the can down the road; we don't have the luxury of time to get the next generation to fix our fiscal problems. If we make tough choices and get our house in order, the United States can compete with the best and brightest in the world. But I'm equally confident that if we don't, this country is on its way to being a second-rate power."
>
> **ERSKINE BOWLES,**
> COCHAIR, NATIONAL COMMISSION ON FISCAL RESPONSIBILITY AND REFORM, AT 2012 ULI SPRING MEETING IN CHARLOTTE, NORTH CAROLINA

> "We are going to have to reinvent the rules to include more transparency and more equity."
>
> **JOSEPH AZRACK,**
> PRESIDENT AND CEO, APOLLO GLOBAL REAL ESTATE, AND MEMBER, ULI BOARD OF DIRECTORS

good time to reexamine assumptions and take note of recent lessons learned.

INTEREST RATE CONUNDRUM

In most countries, rates cannot go much lower—wonderful for those who can score a long-term loan but emblematic of soured economies. Any rational observer figures that rates must revert to the norm eventually, but years of low rates can lull investors into a false sense of security. The United States remains the world's safe haven, but what if global capital seeks alternatives? What happens if property revenue growth fails to keep up with rising capitalization rates? And what about inflation—will governments eventually go to the printer to escape the debt mess? High inflation rates could hamstring economies further. Any pathway to sustainability promises potential land mines, so most players must keep their eyes wide open, execute on risk management strategies, and try not to overextend.

MONITOR CAPITAL

Increased capital flows into the real estate sector can provide liquidity and facilitate deal making, but the commercial sector

INTEREST RATE FORECAST

	2007	2008	2009	2010	2011	2012	2013
Interest rates							
Federal funds rate	4.25%	0.13%	0.13%	0.13%	0.13%	0.13%	0.13%
90-day T-bill rate	4.47%	1.39%	0.15%	0.14%	0.05%	0.10%	0.23%
Treasury yields:							
One-year maturity	4.52%	1.82%	0.47%	0.32%	0.18%	0.20%	0.30%
Ten-year maturity	4.63%	3.67%	3.26%	3.21%	2.79%	1.89%	2.61%
Freddie Mac commitment rates							
Fixed-rate mortgages	6.34%	6.04%	5.04%	4.69%	4.46%	3.78%	4.44%
Adjustable-rate mortgages	5.56%	5.17%	4.71%	3.79%	3.04%	2.80%	2.99%
Prime rate	8.05%	5.09%	3.25%	3.25%	3.25%	3.25%	3.25%

Source: 2012 NAHB/HousingEconomics.
Note: Forecast rates on August 1, 2012. Data are averages of seasonally adjusted quarterly data and may not match annual data published elsewhere.

easily gets overwhelmed by too much capital, precipitating pricing volatility and boom-bust cycles. When capitalization rates head below 5 percent (even in a low interest rate environment), it's usually time to diminish investment appetites, except maybe for the most prime real estate in the very best locations.

LONGER-TERM HOLDS

Opportunistic investing plays well only in a few windows during the real estate cycle. If developers and opportunistic investment managers can raise money, they will always find ways to put it to work, whether market fundamentals make sense or not. Lenders and investors must be the control point and know when to pull back or suffer the consequences of overbuilding and unmet expectations of return.

LOWER EXPECTATIONS

Commercial real estate can reliably deliver an income-based return with modest appreciation—historically in the mid to high single digits. Leverage can boost returns but adds to risk, and easy credit leads to unbalanced markets and even greater risk. Investors need to satisfy themselves with bond-plus returns over longer-term holding periods. Asking for real estate to do more, other than buying at the cyclical

> "Whether or not Greece exits the Eurozone, how we prepare is the most important thing to focus on."
>
> **DAISUKE KITTA,**
> PRINCIPAL, REAL ESTATE GROUP, BLACKSTONE

AVERAGE CAPITALIZATION RATES BY PROPERTY TYPE (PERCENT)

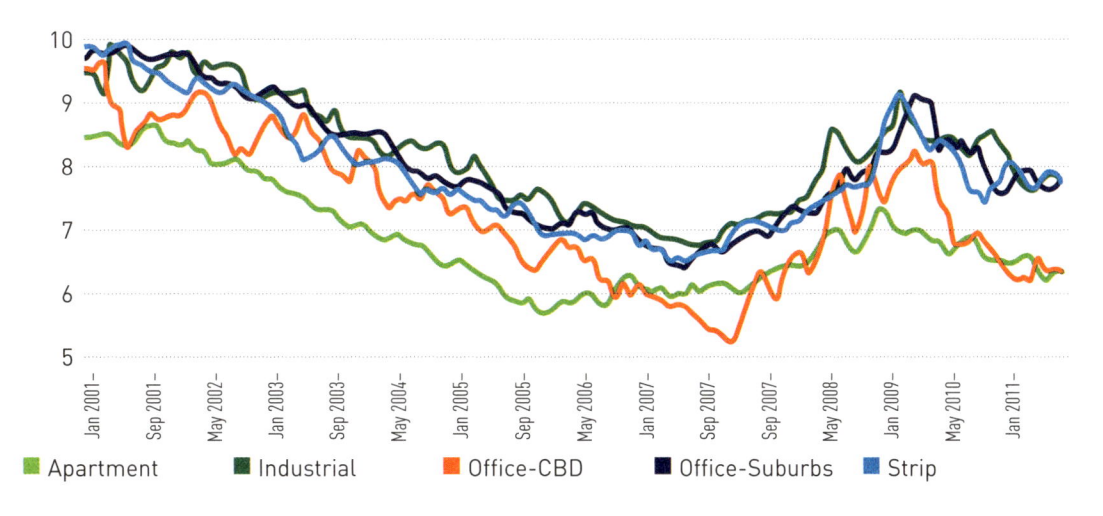

Source: Real Capital Analytics, July 2011.

The legacy of single-use superblock land use planning in Asian cities is being challenged by new mixed-use developments like the recently completed D-Cube City project in Seoul, South Korea.

bottom or developing a project into a demand upswing, usually results in disappointment.

STAY DISCIPLINED

Housing markets will eventually recover—some gateway markets already have, a few other select markets are beginning to rebound—and bottom-feeders can make good deals now. But lender underwriting must remain disciplined, buyers should be required to put adequate equity down, and purchases should be based on buying a home, not making an outsized gain. Lenders and regulators need to avoid gimmicky mortgage structures that encourage consumers to take out loans beyond their means. They must consider whether

Domestic tourism is bringing new vitality to old streets in cities across China.

GLOBAL DOMESTIC TOURISM

Domestic tourism is driving local markets globally. Delivery of hospitality and tourism-related infrastructure—at the correct price point—is a challenge faced across emerging markets throughout Asia and Latin America. Paris, London, and New York remain top global destinations but the other seven in the top ten are located in Asia or the Middle East. Keep watch as the U.S. State Department streamlines the U.S. tourist visa application process and produces untapped demand. As technology facilitates international security, new markets will follow.

Focus on:

INDIA Hospitality markets are experiencing a significant uptick in hotel building throughout the country. Branding matters: Starwood will nearly double its assets to 55 hotels in the next three years and Hyatt has 56 in the development pipeline. Many are located outside conventional gateway markets, such as the Grand Hyatt about to open in Kochi, in the tourist-popular state of Kerala. Best Western's properties include hotels in the smaller cities of Shirdi and Visakhapatnam. Global brands are staking out market share, as Dubai-based Jumeirah is in partnership talks with several Indian operators.

AUSTRALIA Popular among Asian tourists, Australia is fashioning significant growth in Adelaide and other markets beyond the well-beaten path to Sydney harbor.

NEW ORLEANS Look no further than the Big Easy to see how tourism can drive local markets. By 2010 visitors had rebounded to pre-Katrina arrival numbers.

PHILADELPHIA As the convention business hits its stride, business leaders predict that to meet near-term demand this city will need 2,000 additional rooms beyond pipeline projects by Kimpton and Sheraton.

SIGNIFICANT U.S. LOSSES FROM NATURAL CATASTROPHE (1950–2010)

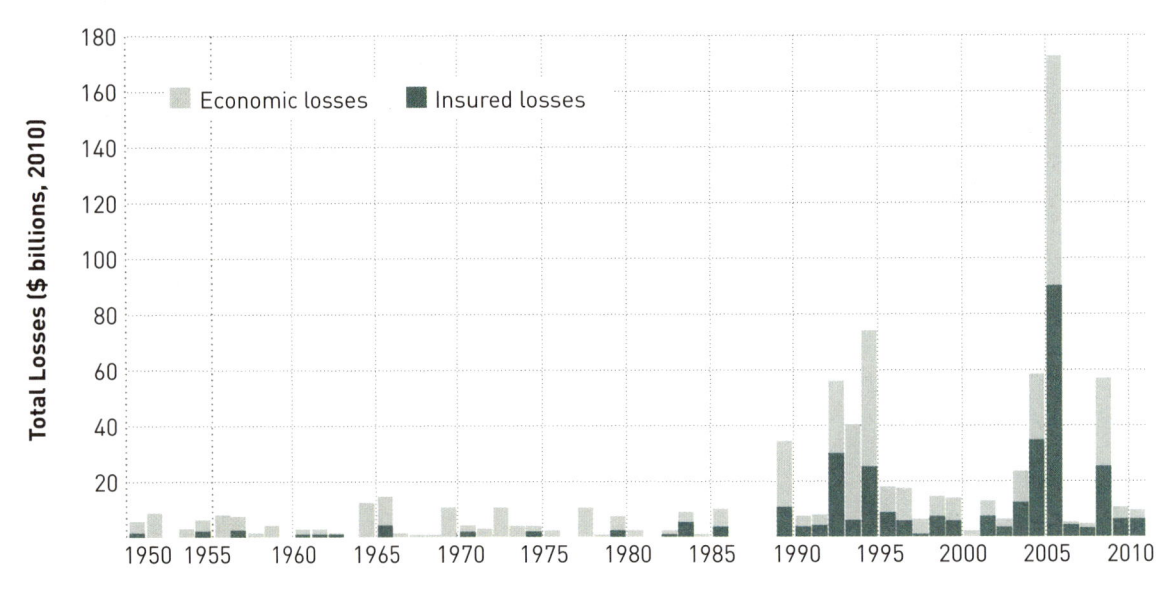

Legend: Economic losses, Insured losses
Y-axis: Total Losses ($ billions, 2010)
X-axis: 1950–2010

Source: NatCat Service, ©Munich RE, 2010.

interest-only terms or reverse mortgages really make sense for most borrowers. In the meantime, long-term deleveraging and lack of personal savings could limit the U.S. homebuyer pool and slow growth in demand for the foreseeable future. At some point, television commercials about get-rich-quick housing seminars will set off warning signals about market overreaching—but televisions may not be in the picture by the time that happens again.

KNOW GLOBAL

Developers understandably will look away from North America and Europe to emerging markets. Consider total worldwide urban population gains of one billion and the need for 90 percent more residential stock by 2025. Some estimates suggest the need for $10 trillion in new investments for commercial and residential buildings and infrastructure over that period. The addition of an estimated 1.8 billion people to the consumer class worldwide will create significant opportunities, homing in on places of growing buying power. In emerging markets, high-income households (above $70,000 annually) will triple to 60 million, a small relative number but one that

"We need more knowledgeable intermediaries who fully comprehend the realities of business risk and reward in the property markets, while also understanding what it takes to improve the quality of life for our urbanizing populations."

HIS HIGHNESS THE AGA KHAN,
2011 ULI NICHOLS PRIZE WINNER, AND FOUNDER AND CHAIRMAN OF THE AGA KHAN DEVELOPMENT NETWORK

offers huge potential for spurring real estate opportunities. That's something to be aware of.

INEVITABLE SHOCKS

Dealing with visible risks we can't control will remain the industry's biggest challenge in the lengthy unraveling of the world financial crisis. In perilous times, industry leaders ponder how to operate a business on the edge of a precipice. At any moment, a country default or bank collapse could capsize fragile capital markets, and what can be done about it?

>> **AT THE VERY LEAST, VIGILANCE SHOULD ELIMINATE SURPRISE ABOUT UPCOMING SURPRISES.**

LEADING TO NEXT

▶▶ THE FUTURE SURROUNDS US; IT'S JUST UNEVENLY DISTRIBUTED.

ADJUSTING COURSE

How can the real estate industry take the lead to drive change rather than react to it? After three decades of boom/bust cycles and plenty of market dislocation, it is time to adjust and do some things differently, especially in the face of new and unexpected challenges.

Though buildings and land remain physical assets, fundamentally they are framed in a context of community and region. ULI members and other industry stakeholders have an opportunity to reconsider and refine valuation paradigms beyond today's professional practices and to do so in a manner that acknowledges more issues associated with the context of real estate assets. Technology, affordability, accessibility, operations, and environmental variables can become clearer metrics that are more relevant to investors, builders, and lenders alike. Lenders must remain disciplined and take responsibility for their loan originations, and borrowers must acknowledge and settle for fair value. Over the long haul, appropriate contributions of equity will better protect investors, owners, and lenders alike.

In concert with elected leaders, the industry must help formulate sound infrastructure policy that supports communities and helps spawn myriad private investments in a new age of community building. New transit-oriented development can mitigate congestion and create mixed-use environments with robust local tax bases. Working in concert with planners, policy makers, and community stakeholders, leaders within the real estate industry can be the problem solvers—creatively making places of enduring value.

GETTING AHEAD OF CHANGE

Most market participants measure success in terms of quantity: more is better, even if more inevitably leads to periods of (much) less. Today the industry should strive to maintain mar-

> "Executives need to be implementing leadership programs necessary to attract, motivate, and retain the best and brightest minds in real estate. Individual companies and the industry can benefit by acting strategically, proactively, and decisively to plan for who's up next and to cultivate those young professionals with leadership qualities."
>
> **PETER RUMMELL,**
> CHAIRMAN, ULI

> "Patience is key and there are no quick fixes. It's going to be a hard, long grind to work through the current market challenges."
>
> **SIMON TREACY,**
> ULI TRUSTEE AND CHAIRMAN, ULI SOUTH ASIA, AND GROUP CHIEF EXECUTIVE, MGPA

kets in relative equilibrium. With a deluge of information available today about demographics, employment, the environment, and technology, decision makers are able to craft insightful and future-oriented strategies in an unprecedented manner. The ability and capacity to forge better communities—and better returns—depends on developing a shared vision and shared metrics to measure progress.

Getting ahead of change means taking the lead to innovate and change course. It is time to accept greater accountability to address the challenges ahead by providing leadership to sustain thriving communities. Join ULI in this worldwide endeavor as we leverage our network of land use professionals to solve problems in this great era of city building.

> "In a world transformed by technology and economic globalization, the world's cities need ULI's wisdom now more than ever."
>
> **FORMER PRESIDENT WILLIAM JEFFERSON CLINTON**
> AT ULI'S 2012 HONOR AWARD CEREMONY AT THE NATIONAL BUILDING MUSEUM IN WASHINGTON, D.C.

ACKNOWLEDGMENTS

This publication has been directly informed by ULI member dialogue from ULI programs conducted by ULI District Councils and other special events around the world. We deeply appreciate the input and participation of ULI trustees, members, and staff who participated in the dialogues and meetings used to create this publication. We are especially grateful to those members who contributed their time and insights during dedicated research retreats.

Special gratitude is extended to the thousands of ULI members who participated in 2011–2012 dedicated What's Next? programs:

- **2011 ULI Fall Meeting What's Next? Full Member Workshop Participants**

- **2012 ULI Spring Meeting What's Next? Full Member Workshop Participants**

- **2011–12 Dedicated ULI District Council Programs Exploring What's Next?**
  Atlanta, Boston, Central Florida, Cleveland, Dallas (North Texas), Houston, Memphis, New Mexico, North Florida, Philadelphia, Portland, San Antonio, San Diego, Seattle, South Carolina, Southeast Florida/Caribbean, Southwest Florida, Tampa Bay, Washington, D.C.

- **ULI Survey of District Councils, Summer 2012**
  Arizona, Atlanta, Austin, Boston, Central Florida, Charlotte, Chicago, Cincinnati, Colorado, Columbus, Houston, Idaho, Los Angeles, Michigan, Minnesota, Nashville, New Mexico, New York, North Florida, North Texas, Northwest, Orange County/Inland Empire, Philadelphia, Sacramento, San Diego/Tijuana, San Francisco, South Carolina, St. Louis, Tampa Bay, Toronto, Triangle, Washington

- **New York City ULI Regional Seminar**

- **San Francisco ULI Regional Seminar**

Special gratitude is extended to all ULI staff who contributed to research and production of What's Next? programs.

PROJECT DIRECTORS

Maureen L. McAvey
Senior Resident Fellow, ULI/Bucksbaum Family Chair for Retail

Uwe Brandes
Senior Vice President, Initiatives

LEAD AUTHOR

Jonathan D. Miller

PROJECT STAFF

Sarah Nemecek
Project Manager

Stephanie Ball
Project Researcher

Jonathan P. Katz
Research Assistant

ULI SENIOR RESIDENT FELLOWS

Stephen R. Blank
Senior Resident Fellow
Finance and Capital Markets

John K. McIlwain
Senior Resident Fellow
J. Ronald Terwilliger Chair for Housing

Edward T. McMahon
Senior Resident Fellow
ULI/Charles Fraser Chair on Sustainable Development

Maureen McAvey
Senior Resident Fellow
ULI/Bucksbaum Family Chair for Retail

Tom Murphy
Senior Resident Fellow
ULI/Klingbeil Family Chair for Urban Development

ULI SENIOR EXECUTIVES

Patrick Phillips
Chief Executive Officer

Cheryl Cummins
Executive Officer

Michael Terseck
Chief Financial Officer/Chief Administrative Officer

Richard M. Rosan
President, ULI Foundation

Joe Montgomery
Chief Executive, ULI Europe

David Howard
Executive Vice President, Development and ULI Foundation

Lela Agnew
Executive Vice President, Communications

Marilee Utter
Executive Vice President, District Councils

ULI PRODUCTION STAFF

James Mulligan
Senior Editor

Lise Lingo, Publications Professionals
Manuscript Editor

Betsy VanBuskirk
Creative Director

Anne Morgan
Graphic Designer

Craig Chapman
Senior Director, Publishing Operations